Four Benefits
of the Liturgy

A Benedictine monk

Four Benefits
of the Liturgy

The Saint Austin Press
MCMXCIX

THE SAINT AUSTIN PRESS
296 Brockley Road
London   SE4 2RA
Tel   +44 (0) 181 692 6009
Fax   +44 (0) 181 469 3609

Email: books@saintaustin.org
http://www.saintaustin.org

From a lecture delivered by Dom Gérard Calvet OSB
to the first colloquium of CIEL, 1995.
Published in book form, in French, by Éditions Sainte Madeleine, 1996.

ISBN 1 901157 08 3

Designed and printed by NEWTON Design & Print

CONTENTS

INTRODUCTION

The young people who come on retreat to the monastery often wonder why we give so much importance to the liturgy in our monastic lives. One of our novices, now a monk and a priest, who underwent harsh trials during his noviciate, supplies the answer. One day he confided: "I would not have persevered in my vocation if God had not, by the grace of the holy liturgy, given me a helping hand each day during the course of the year." This, to a greater or lesser extent, is an experience shared in all our monasteries. In the very depths of our souls the liturgy works a sort of seductive charm. Day after day a voice makes itself heard with a sweetness and an aptness which cannot be mistaken, enlightening souls from within by a succession of light touches.

From this, one will see that the liturgy is essential to the monastic vocation; it is a natural unfolding of the grace of baptism. If there is an initial happiness in realising oneself eternally incorporated into the family of the children of God, there is also another happiness, that of becoming an exalter of the divine glory and of receiving, as if in advance, some ray of this light

11

from up above. It is in this way that the monk, by means of symbols, signs, sacraments and sacramentals enters into the jubilation of the Church through the sacred drama of the age old liturgy, sung in Latin to the melodies of Gregorian chant. If it were necessary to sum up all the benefits that daily participation in the public prayer of the Church brings us, we would distill them down to four essential points:

- the continual recalling of the transcendence of God
- the attractive power of liturgical beauty
- the sense of the Church
- the education of the inner man

THE TRANSCENDENCE OF GOD

Man is only truly himself when he adores. Adoration is the sign by which the creature identifies himself and performs his primary function. For thousands of years humanity has blindly groped for God and despite unimaginable errors it has invariably showed itself loyal to the austere duty of adoration. Perhaps man often combined plenty of servile fear in his appproach to the divinity. But there was, all the same, the humble recognition of a bond of dependence where not everything rang false: the religion of antiquity had in its favour that it was still waiting. One remembers the famous episode of the altar dedicated to *the unknown God,* of which St Paul made use in order to enter into dialogue with the Athenians. (Acts 17:23). It would seem that God prefers to be adored without being known, than to be known without being adored, because in the latter case we would be dealing with a false knowledge, with a belittled and mistaken idea of the divinity. One recognises, of course, in this all the drama of the modern world.

How does one define adoration? It is, in the broadest sense, a free and loving submission of the whole being to the divine transcendence, by which the believer recognises the sovereign rights God has over his creature. But Revelation adds to this a new understanding that represents something of a watershed in man's concept of God.

Firstly the idea of the supernatural: the divinity now ceases to appear as a superior force situated at the summit of the forces of nature. Instead, the divinity is situated on a plane infinitely *superior* to the forces of nature. We must not allow this word to become banal: supernatural is not a synonym for unusual or for marvellous. It refers to a reality which is infinitely above the natural conceptions of sanctity that man is capable of having. The word *sanctus* means separated. Our Lord speaks forcefully of this in the Gospels: "You are from below, I am from above. You are of this world, I am not of this world." (John 8:23)

Following on from this, the second effect of Revelation is that this God, three times holy, reveals himself as Father: far from crushing or terrifying, he raises his creature to the dignity of a son. Adoration does not exclude tenderness, then: such is the power of the liturgy.

Forgetfulness of God's transcendence has plunged the world into a tragic situation. It is the beginning of that great apostasy announced by the Scriptures. The state of the world today, however, is worse than that of antiquity: its rejection of God makes it the world of refusal rather than just the world of expectation. The present world is dying because it has rid itself of the supernatural. The cult of man, social hypertrophy, the affirmation of self; who can pretend that this naturalism has not entered into modern man's manner of prayer? It appears under the most varied forms: a raging hunger for novelty and adaptation; the invasion of modern music and vulgar language; lack of education which drowns the unchanging prayer of the Bride of Christ in that ever-rolling stream which is the sensibility of the day; and finally *creativity* which is one of the subtlest forms of human pride. In short, modern man gives in to the temptation to adapt religion to man instead of doing what the Church has tried to do down the ages: to adapt man to religion.

Turning our backs resolutely on these naturalistic tendencies, it should be easy to see that liturgical expression, because it transcends the fashions and particularities of time and place, is - in essence, and by God's design - perfectly adapted to that which man carries most profoundly and essentially within himself: the instinct for the sacred and the thirst for adoration. That which never mounts up towards

15

God will never descend towards man. "He that is of the earth, of the earth he is, and of the earth he speaketh." (John 3:31). The language of the liturgy has to come down from God before we can expect it to make us ascend towards Him.

As a remedy for these deviations, the Church offers us the theocentrism of her prayer. Altar, priest and faithful must turn in a spirit of adoration towards the infinite majesty of God. Our liturgy is essentially about adoration. The "mass facing the people" is largely incapable of expressing this. "There is a danger," says Cardinal Ratzinger, "when the communitarian character tends to transform the assembly into a closed circle. It is necessary to react with all one's strength against the idea of an autonomous and self-sufficient community: the community must not enter into dialogue with itself; it is a collective force turned towards the coming Lord." (*The Ratzinger Report*)

The readers of the epistle and the gospel stand facing the faithful who listen to them. What could be more normal? But then, at the beginning of the sacrificial part of the mass, the celebrant goes up to the altar and, turned towards the thrice holy God, he offers the propitiatory victim. At the *Te igitur*, the priest lifts his eyes towards the cross and makes a deep, reverent and adoring bow. He is turned towards the east, facing the crucified Lord who is also the

Lord of glory, because it is from the east that the Son of Man will return, surrounded by angels, with great power and great majesty.

This facing towards the East has a second aspect: each morning the celebrant turns towards the rising sun, the most beautiful cosmic image of the risen Christ, eternally begotten of the Father, and unceasingly and victoriously reborn in the hearts of the baptised. The silence of the Canon, when it follows on from the chant of the choir, is a silence of adoration where the created word disappears before the Creator. The first benefit of the liturgy, then, is its theocentrism. As Father Bouyer said: "How greatly it is to be desired that Christianity should once more come to discover this primary meaning of the Mass: its theocentric meaning, and the reorientation of the whole of mankind, of the whole universe, towards its true centre: this universal return, wrought in Christ crucified and ascended up to heaven; this resumption of all things in the immense flood of divine love, flowing back finally in filial love towards its source, the Father."

(The Meaning of the Monastic Life)

THE ATTRACTIVE POWER
OF LITURGICAL BEAUTY

But adoration does not imply annihilation. The beauty of the sacred rites enobles souls. It elevates them by exercising over them the sweet attraction of Heaven. Real tradition is not sad. Sunday masses at the Abbey show this clearly. For two hours, no one, neither infant nor adolescent shows any sign of impatience. Why? MacNabb, a historian of religions, gives us the response; he says that one enters the Church by two doors: the door of the intelligence and the door of beauty. The narrow door, he says, is that of the intelligence; it is open to intellectuals and scholars. The wider door is that of beauty. Henri Charlier said, in the same vein: "It is necessary to lose the illusion that the truth can communicate itself fruitfully without that splendour that is of one nature with it and which is called beauty." *(L'Art et la Pensée)*

The Church in her impenetrable mystery as bride of Christ, the *Kyrios* of Glory, has need of an earthly epiphany (ie. manifestation) accessible to all: this is the majesty of her temples, the splendour of her liturgy and the sweetness of her chants. Take a group of Japanese tourists visiting Notre Dame Cathedral in Paris. They look at the height of the archways, the splendour of the stained-glass windows, the harmony of the proportions. Suppose that at that moment, sacred ministers dressed in orphried velvet copes enter in procession for solemn Vespers. The visitors watch in silence; they are entranced: beauty has opened its doors to them. Now the *Summa Theologica* of St Thomas Aquinas and Notre Dame in Paris are products of the same era. They say the same thing. But who among the visitors has read the *Summa* of St Thomas? The same phenomenon is found at all levels. The tourists who visit the Acropolis in Athens are confronted with a civilisation of beauty. But who among them can understand Aristotle?

And so it is with the beauty of the liturgy. More than anything else it deserves to be called *the splendour of the truth*. It opens to the small and the great alike the treasures of its magnificence: the beauty of psalmody, sacred chants and texts, candles, harmony of movement and dignity of bearing. With sovereign art the liturgy exercises a truly seductive influence on souls, whom it touches directly, even before the spirit perceives its influence. But it is a delicate art, diametrically opposed to a certain kind of post-conciliar liturgy "rendered opaque and boring, thanks to its taste for the banal and the mediocre, to the point of making one shudder." (*The Ratzinger Report*) We also fear the breed of activists who meddle with the liturgy by introducing novelties in order to render it more attractive. It is once more Cardinal Ratzinger who warns us: "The liturgy is not a show, a spectacle requiring briliant producers and talented actors. The life of the liturgy does not consist in 'pleasant' surprises and attractive 'ideas' but in solemn repetitions." *(Ibid)*

Let us say a few words about solemnity. Above all we must not confuse it with decorum. Far from weighing us down, the solemn nature of the rites is designed to express clearly the brilliance of the superatural. As long as it has reached a certain loftiness, all sacred liturgy tends, by means of ritual, to raise us above the banal and the everyday, not for the sake of an aesthetic goal, but to show the faithful that the action taking place comes from God. This majestic unfolding of the liturgy has no other end. It signifies that something heavenly comes to touch the earth. St Gregory, the great Benedictine pope of the sixth century, wrote in his *Dialogues*: "At the hour of the sacrifice, the heavens, on hearing the voice of the priest, open; in this mystery of Jesus Christ, the choirs of angels are present, that which is above joins with that which is below, Heaven and Earth unite, the visible and the invisible are made one." (IV, 60)

The solemnity of worship is an integral part of the Catholic liturgy and has to be cultivated as an element of its very message, always on condition that this solemnity does not degenerate into pomposity and affectation. Adornment, after all, succeeds most supremely when it blends in so well that it is itself forgotten. Accusations of triumphalism are an insult to the joy of the poor who love to see greatness exalted. Here again are Cardinal Ratzinger's thoughts on the matter: "There is no trace of triumphalism in the solemnity with which the Church expresses the glory of God, the joy of the faith, the victory of truth and light over error and darkness. The richness of the liturgy is not the richness of some priestly caste; it is the richness of all, including the poor, who infact desire it and are by no means scandalised by it." (ibid)

There can hardly be a more enlightening example of the power which the beauty of the liturgy has to effect conversions than that contained in the richly evocative *Chronicles of Nestor*. The Chronicles tell us that how Prince Vladimir of Kiev, still a pagan, wanted to worship the one God, and so listened to Muslims, Jews and Greeks, each of whom came to show him their religion. He sent a delegation of ten men to go and see with their own eyes how each of the groups practised their liturgy.

Having visited various mosques in Bulgaria, they arrived in Constantinople.

"The Byzantine Emperor," Nestor tells us, "sent a message to the Patriarch saying: 'Some Russians have come with the intention of studying our religion; prepare your church and your clergy and put on your pontifical vestments so that they will see the glory of our God.' The patriarch called for his clergy; they celebrated the solemnities according to custom, they burnt incense, and the choir sang. The emperor went to the Basillica with the Russians and had them seated where they had a good view; then he showed them the beauties of the church, of the chant, of the service conducted by the bishop and the ministry of the deacons and explained to them the divine liturgy. (...) Having returned to their country they told their prince: *First we visited the Bulgarians and saw how they worshipped in their temples; they stand upright without a belt; they bow, they sit down, looking all around like men possessed, and there is no joy among them, but an awful sadness and stench. Their religion is not good ... It was then that we went to Greece and they led us to the place where they worship their God. From that moment on we did not know if we were in heaven or on earth; there is no other sight like it here below, and there is nothing of such beauty. We simply cannot describe it; all we know is that it is there that God lives amongst men; and their worship is more marvellous than in the other countries.*"

The message is not difficult to grasp. The liturgy does more than just describe to us the wonders of our heavenly homeland. It pushes ajar the doors of the Kingdom of Heaven. Man enters there body and soul: he sees it, he hears it, he smells it, everything speaks to him of God. But how many of our contemporaries and even, alas, how many sons and daughters of the Church, know that they have here the golden key to Paradise?

A SENSE OF THE CHURCH

That which theologians call the *sensus Ecclesiae* is a supernatural sensitivity through which the faithful feel as if by intuition whether something is in conformity with the faith and with the tradition of the Church. It is a bit like the way in which the children of a family sense whether something is in keeping or out of keeping with the spirit of the house: "our family does not do things like that," they say. In the same way, the "sense of the Church" is not the product of didactic teaching. It is the effect of a superior instinct, often found more deeply amongst the poorest people, whom the age-old practice of the liturgy enlightens from within in order to make them understand how to bear witness to their faith, even in the prescence of those more intellectual than themselves.

It is sometimes asked how it was that the faith was maintained during periods of persecution, especially in parts of the world where religion is deprived of its external means of expression, such as with the freedom of the press or preaching. Here is what Maximus V, the Malachite Patriarch, said to the first synod of bishops (1977) dedicated to catechesis: "It was the celebration of the divine liturgy that kept the faith of the faithful intact during the centuries of Muslim persecution."

The same phenomenon can be observed in the countries of the East: Baptism and the Eucharist constituted the unique but irrepressible support for the faith, a support that clashed with the communist machine. We touch here on the social and missionary character of the liturgy: the ministry it exerts is one of gathering around a fixed point. It prevents the faithful from sliding down the slippery slope of forgetfulness, it prevents them from drifting away from the faith. "It is," says Dom Guéranger, "tradition at its highest degree of power and solemnity." On several occasions the Abbot of Solesmes cites Bossuet's description of the liturgy as the "main instrument of Tradition", showing that it can be called "Tradition professed" as opposed to the declarations of the councils which represent "Tradition defined." Father Clérissac recounts that during the middle-ages a Jew asked to be baptised because he had noticed that the lyricism of the synagogue was surpassed by that of the liturgy of the Church. For the Church of Christ to distinguish itself from other religions, it is necessary for its prayer and its sacraments to surround themselves with a veil sufficiently transparent to allow the mystery of their origins to be guessed. There is a profound reason for having a sacred language: not only does it express the universality of a religion but it serves as a fixed point of reference in the ever-moving stream of history.

The popes know very well that the people do not read their encyclicals. When Pius XI wrote *Quas Primas*, his great encyclical on Christ the King, his intention was to fight what he callled the *pest of secularism*. Now the text of the encyclical itself contained the announcement of a new feast in honour of the social kingship of the Redeemer. Here is how Pius XI justified the introduction of this Mass, unknown until then, into the cycle of the liturgical year: "In the task of helping the truths of the faith reach the people and of raising them to the joys of the interior life, the annual solemnities of the liturgical feasts are much more effective than all the documents, even the most serious, of the Church's magisterium: the latter are usually only read by a small number of the most cultured; the salutary influence of the former reaches the heart and the intelligence, and thus the whole man."

One notices here the close link which unites the faith and the liturgy. With the liturgy I enter into the being of the Church, into its innermost sanctuary. I see that it comes from God, and therefore that it knows better than me how to believe, how to speak to God, and how to conduct oneself before the divine Majesty. And when I say the *amen* which concludes a liturgical prayer I subscribe to an objective thought which I make mine and which surpasses me infinitely. It is in this way that, little by little, we acquire a supernatural instinct which will quite naturally lead the faithful to *sentire cum Ecclesia*: that capacity to feel and think with the Church.

When, after the council, in the terrible years of the 1970s, a destructive clergy discarded genuflections, sacred rites, Gregorian Chant and reverence for the angels and saints, what saved the faith of the Christian people was the love of these holy things. It was a love which the liturgy had enkindled in their hearts. And the Church herself, so under fire, and sometimes, alas, so misrepresented - how can we safeguard our admiration and love for her if not by the sweet and continuous influence of her prayer and her sacraments? It is there that we recognise her as Virgin and Mother, composed of sinners but without sin, immersed in time but belonging already to eternity thanks to the attraction exercised over his Body by the Head, Christ Himself, enthroned in glory.

How are the faithful and the unbelieving supposed to recognise the face of *Ecclesia Mater*,

Mother Church, if she does not constantly show what we could call her *power of sanctification?* Dom Vonier has said: "The power which the Catholic Church possesses to sanctify is truly prodigious; she makes no secret of it; she proclaims it to the whole world; she fulfills her special mission, in a magnificent manner, as queen of the spiritual world. The consecration or dedication of a church is a kind of counterbalance, inspired by God, to the efforts of the unclean spirit, which Christ has outlined for us in the Gospels. The Church launches an assault on the stupendous material construction [ie. the imposing church building], she enters into it in glory and in grace, and she invites her children to follow her and find rest for their souls in a house set aside for holiness." *(Christianus)*

If we question converts to Catholicism, their testimonies always follow the same pattern: "The young man I was at 18 years old, who was searching amidst a great cloud for a truth which presented itself to him confusedly - a living truth, made for the soul and not just for the mind - had sanctity revealed to him by Gregorian chant. In its bareness and its simplicity Gregorian chant took me much further than secular music, it allowed me to catch a glimpse of mysteries which I never suspected; it filled me with this 'plenitude of God' of which St Paul speaks; it told me that this plenitude was there for me if I wanted it; I was certain that it was God Himself who spoke to me through this chant." (André Charlier, *Le Chant Gregorien*)

Dom Grammont, at the end of a solemn high Mass attended by a group of Protestant ministers, noticed one of them, overwhelmed, making his way towards him exclaiming: "I have seen the Church!" He had seen the Church through the display of its purest and most ancient tradition. It is by the words, the chants and the unchanging rituals of the liturgy that the Christian soul finds itself put back in touch with a homeland which transcends the centuries.

THE EDUCATION OF THE INNER MAN

That which is most hidden and most secret within us, that which hides itself from view, and which gives life its meaning, the precious pearl, the treasure hidden in the field, that which the contemplatives search for and having found it would not exchange for all the gold in the world, such is the discovery of God within us.

The greatest benefit of the liturgy, and its most profound reason for existing - because sacred beauty is not an end in itself - is to lead us, with a steady hand, into the sanctuary of the soul, where the only drama essential to human existence unfolds: the growth of our supernatural life.

With the exception of the Carmelites, those angels of heaven imprisoned in time, who have a special vocation to search for God without the help of images, most of us must draw from the immense treasury of signs, words and ritual actions in order to nourish our meditations. For two thousand years the Church has taught her children the difficult art of prayer aided not by human industry but by means of a divine pedagogy of which she has the secret.

A taste for interior or mental prayer and for silent prayer is not acquired by a process of reasoning; it is by learning to merge the interior movement of our soul with that of the Bride of Christ that one enters into the mystery of the Godhead.

Let us read what an Abbot says to his monks: "Prayer, such as it was understood by St. Benedict, has as its theme the very text of the *Opus Dei* [the work of God, i.e. the Divine Office]. It springs up from the womb of this Office. Let yourself be caught up in it. Afterwards, continue to draw on what you have gathered during the Office. God is bowing down to you at this moment. In silence, question the ideas that have been planted in this way. This kind of interior prayer is the most intimate part of the *Opus Dei* during its celebration; it becomes afterwards its reveberating echo, a precious perfume, a personal fruit suited to the dispositions and needs of each one of us according to the promptings of the Holy Spirit. Because the *Opus Dei* takes place seven times a day and once each night the river of prayer flows unceasingly amongst the children of St Benedict, and the soul that remains constantly on this blessed shore, may drink there, in long drafts, in such a way as to feel, from morning to evening and from evening to morning, its salutary freshness." (Dom Romain Banquet, *La Doctrine Monastique*)

Dom Delatte speaks in similar terms. Calling to mind *L'Annee Liturgique*, which was the great work of Dom Guéranger, he underlines in a few words the secret of the influence of the liturgy: "Assuredly revolutions make more noise, the works of man are often more instantly noticeable, whereas the supernatural good makes itself known without noise and hides itself in silence. But who can know the sweet and tranquil effect of this universal teaching? Souls, when they have once tasted it, cannot take themselves away from it, as if they recognise there the imprint of the Church and the savour of their baptism." As regards meditation on liturgical texts, it can be defined in a short phrase: *From the lips and the heart of the Church, we gather the thoughts of God.*

This is not only true for religious but also for lay people. George Bernanos, very much a man of his time, was a living illustration of this: his interior life was drawn to the sources of the liturgy, and he was transformed from being a brilliant pamphleteer to being a writer of the soul. This is described vividly by Bruckberger: "Each day he read the newspaper and listened to the radio. However each morning, whatever happened, he set aside half an hour as sacred.

33

Before his family awoke, before the house filled with noise, he would read, in his old, worn missal, the Mass of the day in Latin, with all the concentration of mind and soul he was capable of: this predestined soul had received the divine privilege of attention. He nourished himself avidly with the unchanging formulas of the liturgy, finding in them each morning a note of startling freshness. It was as if, each morning, these words were being said for the first time in the entire history of the world and to him alone. They were his daily and supersubstantial bread. It was in this way that he started his day. On Sunday he went to Mass with his family and usually received communion." (*Bernanos Vivant*).

But the education of the inner man is not solely a result of the calm and recollected atmosphere of the Prayer of the Church. There is the almost sacramental presence, rather like a fully charged battery, of Christ within the mysteries of the liturgical year.

How does one describe these mysteries? They are the actions of Christ Jesus, such as his passion, his ressurection and his ascension, accomplished at a particular point in time, finished for ever with regard to their historicity, but conveyed and prolonged throughout the sacrifical action, just as the light from a star, extinct for thousands of years, continues to shine in the night. In the same way, in the different mysteries, Christ throughout the course of the liturgical year, comes to meet souls, in order to recreate them in His image. Dom Delatte described this work of identification with Christ in admiring terms, exalting "the supernatural beauty, this perfect resemblance to Him which the whole supernatural economy attempts to engrave on the soul, this divine imprint which the swinging of the liturgical pendulum stamps perpetually on our souls." One sees, then, in the unfolding of the liturgical year, not a cold and inert representation of the life of Our Lord, but the irradiation of the very person of the Redeemer bringing to life in each of the faithful the saving action of his passion and of his ascent into glory. It is in this way, concludes St Leo, that that which was visible in the life of our Redeemer has passed into the mysteries: *"Quod itaque Redemptoris nostri conspicuum fuit in sacramenta transivit."*

With the Fathers the words *mysteria* and *sacramenta* are synonymous. They designate a sacred action in which the work of our redemption is rendered present, not merely as a symbol, but as the ritual conveyor of an ineffable reality. This doctrine of the realism of the sacraments is of the greatest interest for the life of prayer. This doctrine was lost sight of during the 16th century because of an insistence on individual and psychological aspects of prayer which was detrimental to an objective piety centred on the mysteries. When the liturgy unfolds the Scriptures to us it does not just tell a story likely to favour personal meditation, which each one of us can engage in afterwards. Instead *it realises the actual presence of the Lord*, with which we are free to communicate throughout the length of that act of worship; it is the Church in her entirety - and we in her - taking part in the death and resurrection of our Saviour. This participation is not the fruit of an effort of the mind or of the imagination; it is objective, that is to say it develops as a result of its own dynamism and is not the fruit of a human action, as is the case with private devotions.

What a broadening of our perspective and what a deepening of our faith this implies if we only, by the esteem we have for the action of the liturgy and for its sovereign efficacy, consent to let it live and accomplish in us the divine work of our redemption. It is then that the judicious choice of scriptural texts and their calm repetition, their power of expression, the art of Gregorian chant, the sacraments and the mysteries of the life of Christ which pass back and forth unceasingly before our eyes, imprint on our souls the image of the Son who transforms them and reconciles them with the Father.

Happy, four times happy, the souls formed in the school of the sacred liturgy! The liturgy is the joy of God and of men. It offers those who wish to accept it a remedy for the sadness of exile and gives us a foretaste of eternity.

Other books from the Benedictine Abbey of Le Barroux,
published in English by The Saint Austin Press:

DISCOVERING THE MASS

A Benedictine monk

IN THE MIDST OF THE LITURGICAL CRISIS WITH WHICH WE ARE ALL too familiar, this little book calmly lays forth the rich liturgical heritage of the traditional Roman Mass. What is a sacrament? What is the Mass? What is the liturgy? After addressing these questions, the author examines the detail, historical origin and meaning of the rites of the Holy Sacrifice of the Mass.

IT IS OUR PRAYER THAT THIS BOOK WILL IN SOME MEASURE HELP the faithful to appreciate and more profoundly to love the Mass, and so contribute to a deepening of what Pope St. Pius X called "that true Christian spirit" whose "indispensable fount ... is the active participation in the holy mysteries and in the public and solemn prayer of the Church."

WITH THIS INTENTION, WE RENEW THE CALL MADE BY DOM Prosper Guéranger over 150 years ago: "Open your hearts, children of the Catholic Church, and come and pray the prayer of your Mother!"

paperback, 120 pages, ISBN 1 901157 06 7, **£9.95**

THE SACRED LITURGY

A Benedictine monk

WELCOMED INTO THE INTIMACY OF A MONASTIC COMMUNITY where the Abbot shares these reflections with his monks, the reader discovers the profound riches contained in the liturgy; how the Church's prayer, marvellously fitted to the rhythm of creation and the great heavenly liturgy, is the most effective means for man to grow in the spiritual life.

paperback, 120 pages, ISBN 1 901157 07 5, **£9.95**